Shy

Hevine and Rodeo

Memory and little mouse spirit
on bottom right

Rufus sees a little dog

Angels
Come in All Shapes
& Sizes

By Hevine Schmidt

Light, Love and gentle paws,

Hevine Schmidt

Turn the Page
PUBLISHING

Published by Turn the Page Publishing LLC
P. O. Box 3179
Upper Montclair, NJ 07043
www.turnthepagepublishing.com

ISBN-13: 978-1-938501-25-8

ISBN ebook-13: 978-1-938501-26-5

Angels Come in All Shapes & Sizes
Library of Congress Control Number 2012950539

PRINTED IN THE UNITED STATES OF AMERICA

Editor Quinten Fletcher
Cover Design by Robin McGeever, McB Design
Photographs Hevine Schmidt

DEDICATION

To my husband, Al, my daughter, Mariah, all my animal family members, and to everyone who loves Mother Nature's majestic creatures as much as I do.

INTRODUCTION

One of the most precious gifts that animals give to the world is their unconditional love. Ever since I was a little girl, it's been my dream to be able to return this gift. My husband, Al, made my dream come true when he helped me to create a private animal sanctuary called Little Feet Ranch.

For many years, we have been blessed to provide a permanent home to over fifty wonderful critters. Although I've always focused on improving the lives of the animals in my care, little did I realize how much my animal companions would, ultimately, improve my life. Even now, as I look back on all the amazing experiences that each special soul has brought to us, I'm filled with awe by each one's profound sense of understanding and infinite love.

My purpose in writing this book was not only to share the unique and intriguing stories of my animals, but to explain how we are all connected. It has been my privilege to show you, through this story, the exceptional nature of some of Earth's creatures.

PROLOGUE

When I was nine-years-old, my mom and I had a cat named Nicholas James. Nicky was a wonderful friend and able protector. Spying a prowler outside our house, Nicky jumped from window to window, following his trail, and alerting us to the danger.

One day, Nicky stopped eating, and we soon discovered he had leukemia. A dark time descended upon our family as we helplessly watched Nicky fade away. The veterinarian did everything he could to try to save him, to no avail.

When Nicky went to the Hereafter, I stayed in my room, and couldn't figure out what to do with the love in my heart that now caused me so much pain. My only comfort came from knowing that Nicky was at peace. I tried my hardest to believe the words my mother whispered as she tucked me in at night, "Everything happens for a reason." But I still had trouble understanding and accepting the loss of my beloved Nicky.

Several nights after we buried our family friend, I was drifting off to sleep as the faint light from the hallway shone through the crack of my bedroom door. Out of the corner of my half-closed eyes, I saw movement. My eyes popped open, and I caught a glimpse of what appeared to be the shadow of a cat gliding across the middle of my wall. Then, it disappeared.

Startled and confused, I sat up and rubbed my eyes, wondering if I was dreaming. But as I replayed the scene in my mind, memories of Nicky flooded my thoughts, and a strange calmness settled over me. Strange, because I wasn't afraid, but rather felt a sense of relief. Was it possible that Nicky had visited me from the other side to say goodbye? Or maybe he was saying hello? I wasn't sure; but, somehow, it felt right in my heart. I snuggled under the covers and drifted into a peaceful sleep. I didn't have another experience like that until I became an adult.

That's when everything changed.

Chapter 1

The photograph had been on my refrigerator door for about two months. It was the only photo I had of my darling cats: Velcro, Echo, and Tinkerbelle. Every day, I lovingly looked at the photo, so proud of all three. Then, one morning, while I was admiring the picture, a clear image of a donkey seemed to jump out at me.

It looked very real. I took the photograph down and placed it under a bright light. Yes, there it was — looking through the window was a brown donkey with a white nose. Frowning, I knew that in order for the donkey to peek into that window, it would have to be nine feet tall! I also knew that absolutely no one in the nearby ranches owned a donkey.

Many years ago, my husband and I had adopted a charming little donkey named Rodeo, who still lives on the ranch today (donkeys have been known to live for 30 years or more). Rodeo is a gray, miniature breed, not anywhere near nine-feet-tall.

When I showed the exceptional picture to family and friends, they encouraged me to share the intriguing true story of my unusual experiences with animal friends.

Chapter 2

Years ago, when Al and I decided to adopt a pig, the first place I contacted was the local humane society. The lady at the rescue shelter said she was surprised by my inquiry because, although they rarely had pigs, a baby piglet had just arrived.

My daughter, Mariah, and I jumped in the car and drove to the shelter and adopted the sweet little potbelly. I placed her in a cat carrier, and we all happily headed back home.

We named her Chance. From the beginning, we didn't have any problems with her accepting us as her family, but she did have a few physical and emotional issues. For instance, at the humane society, I noticed she had very dry skin. The lady at the shelter told me that Chance's previous owner had fed her dog food and her dry skin probably resulted from a food allergy. Al and I put her on a proper diet of specially made potbelly pig food and her skin quickly improved.

My husband and I constructed a home for Chance in a fenced in area with shelter, water and shade. Inside our house, we made her a nice, comfy place by the couch where she could sleep and get belly rubs.

At first all was well as we happily welcomed Chance into our family and our home. We potty trained her and taught her to turn in a circle using Cheerios as the reward. Chance would run about the house whenever music was playing; country music was her favorite (the Dixie Chicks to be specific).

At first, Chance was such an enjoyment and a great addition to our family, but then, to our dismay and embarrassment, she grew aggressive; frequently destroying our possessions. One morning, I even had to explain to Mariah's teacher that our pig had eaten Mariah's homework! Chance also became intolerant of anyone else's presence in our home except that of her "family," which only included Al, Mariah, and me. We had to watch her at all times because she was fast as lightning and seemed to enjoy attacking anyone who entered our home. Needless to say, we didn't have many visitors.

Despite her misbehavior, it grew increasingly difficult to persuade Chance to go outside. By nature, pigs are not solitary animals. Chance must have felt that she was already an established part of our family and refused to be parted from us. We made a mistake when we allowed Chance to settle in our house which resulted in her boredom and destruction of our property.

The two cats we had at the time, Velcro and Echo, tiptoed around Chance and tried to stay out of her way. As cats are skilled in stealth, they were successful. However, I now believe that the stress Chance caused in the household contributed to the development of Echo's chronic urinary condition. He was given medication, and his cat food was switched to a prescription-only brand. But it was up to me to correct the stress.

I found a wonderful woman named Jamie, who was a Professional Animal Communicator and known for helping animals with various emotional and physical problems. Through her experience and after watching the interactions of the cats with Chance, she validated to Echo that Chance was a major part of his stress. Jamie also provided valuable tips on how we could help Echo. One remedy was to put a drop of natural homeopathic flower essence in his water bowl daily, to reduce his anxiety. Echo's issues decreased dramatically and, to me, his improvement seemed like a miracle. To Jamie, it was just another day of providing animals what they needed to be healthy and happy.

Jamie also helped to break Echo's habit of drinking from Chance's water dish. I thought this sharing of water was unsanitary, so I gave Jamie a call, and I was completely floored when, after speaking to him only once, Echo never touched Chance's water again.

After Jamie's work with Echo, Chance slipped on the kitchen floor and injured herself. Our farm vet came to the house to assess her condition and she gave us a shocking diagnosis: Chance had suffered an irreversible injury to her lower back. The vet recommended that Chance be euthanized, because she would never be able to walk again.

Knowing the final decision rested with us, Al and I walked outside and, through tears, I told Al it was the right thing to do. Even though Chance had given us so much trouble, she had wound her way into our hearts. Once again, I felt like I was nine, only this time, I was deciding whether my Chance should live or die.

I called Jamie for support as the lethal medication was being prepared. Mariah was at school, and we knew there would be a difficult discussion when she returned home because, even with all of Chance's antics, they shared a special connection.

Al and I knelt down beside Chance, attempting to comfort her.

"Don't be afraid," I told her, stroking her behind the ears. "It's okay to let go." I wanted to say more, but the words caught in my throat.

Chance gave me a knowing look, as if she somehow understood and was returning the love we felt for her. Then the vet inserted the needle, and we watched the light fade from Chance's eyes. Velcro had been perched on the couch, watching Chance without blinking. But after the vet administered the medicine, Velcro hopped off the couch and meandered away.

We were crushed. As ornery and stubborn as Chance had been, we loved her deeply, and now were lost without her. But Chance soon found a way to remind me that she wasn't really gone after all.

Just as sometimes people smell their grandmother's perfume or their father's pipe, one afternoon shortly after Chance crossed, I smelled her scent and I could almost feel her standing next to me. Except, as soon as I smiled and without words acknowledged her presence, the feeling and her smell vanished.

"Chance?" I whispered. And her pungent, familiar odor returned!

I remembered Nicky and thought how lucky I was to know my beloved animals could visit from the Other Side.

To this day, I still catch a whiff of Chance from time to time, which makes me smile, because I think she is aware of how comforted I am by her spiritual connection and her infinite love.

Chapter 3

Animals connect with us in many ways. They can be hilarious or even so irritating at times. Our husky, shepherd, wolf mix, Buzz, decided he needed attention one day, and pooped one lone turd in my handbag. I'm still not over it.

Or, I remember the time I heard a cackle and a ruffle of feathers coming from the barn. When I entered to see what caused the odd noise, I found our goat Capra, grooming a chicken! The goat licked the chicken around its head and under its neck and both Capra and the chicken behaved as if this was quite normal. I couldn't quite catch my breath from laughing.

I believe animals are able to sense illness and perhaps even help in relieving pain. Several years ago, I ruptured a disc in my neck while doing farm chores. After having surgery to fuse two vertebrae together, I was incapacitated for four long months. One day, Echo jumped onto my lap and stared at my neck. He sat there, unmoving, his gaze so intent I was slightly unnerved. Then he climbed up onto my chest, put his paws on my shoulders, and buried his face in my neck.

My neck began to feel warm and tingly. A few minutes later, Echo began to purr, and in an instant my pain subsided. Maybe it was his energy, maybe his soft fur. Whatever happened, I knew the loving touch of an animal helped me.

I remembered watching a television show about dogs who could detect cancer. Could Echo detect health problems as well? Did he somehow know that my neck was injured? I wasn't sure, but Echo seemed to be enjoying himself, and my neck felt great, so we made it our ten-minute daily routine.

At that time, Echo and Velcro were the only two cats in my life. Velcro was ten years older than Echo, and she had been with me since I was a teenager. She stood out from other cats because she was born without a tail. Anyone spending a few moments petting her could easily see her gentle soul and quiet nature, but these attributes didn't reveal how wise she really was. Velcro had always befriended every animal that came to the ranch, and for some reason she was aware of when each one was going to pass away. About a day or so before an animal's time to cross over, Velcro would stay near and constantly stare with her big owl eyes. This happened several times, including just before Chance passed away.

I wondered if it could be possible that Velcro saw something change around an animal that was about to pass. And when I caught her staring at the space above my own head, I was nervous for a moment, but began to wonder if Velcro could see an aura around the living that humans could not.

Then Velcro began doing something very unusual: she meowed right before the phone would ring. I wondered if her sense and ability to anticipate phone calls was similar to the ability of animals to sense when an earthquake is about to happen. I didn't understand how or why it happened, I just tried to keep an open mind.

Chapter 4

One February afternoon, I made the decision to bring another cat home. I was confident that my wise Velcro kitty wouldn't mind a new friend, but I was careful to give Echo extra love any time a newly-rescued animal was introduced to our family. The new kitten's name was Tinkerbelle. We affectionately called her Tink and she stole my heart.

There was a chill in the air the evening we found Tink. My family and I watched the setting sun disappear behind the mountain range as we drove down the rutty dirt road toward home. Suddenly, the car in front of us swerved just missing a small object in the middle of the road. Al pulled over, and I got out of the truck to see what the other driver had narrowly avoided.

Coming closer, I realized it was a kitten.

The kitten just sat there, unmoving, as if she was waiting for me. Without hesitation, I unzipped my coat and carefully placed the kitten inside. She offered no resistance. With my precious cargo, I hurried back to the warmth of the truck. Once inside, I saw that the poor darling's eyes were glued shut with infection and that her ribs were clearly visible. I then understood how desperate her situation was.

By the time we arrived home, I had already given her the name Tinkerbelle. We worked fast to convert an extra bedroom into her new home to give her a chance to recover before meeting the other animals. When I brought her a hearty bowl of soft food, she ate ravenously and then fell into a deep, deep slumber until morning.

I had decided to keep Tink the moment I lifted her from the road. Since my farm vet didn't do spays, I called another veterinarian in town and made an appointment for the next day. He examined Tink and determined

that she was 2½ to 3 months old. She was
also neglected, malnourished, had a terrible
eye infection, and a little scab on her ear. But
he said that she would recover quickly with
good care. He vaccinated her, gave me a tube
of antibiotic eye ointment, and sent us on our
way.

As we drove home, I had a nagging feeling
there might be more kittens in the same area
where we found Tink. After making sure that
Tink was full and comfortable in her new
home, I searched for hours for Tink's litter
mates, but I didn't see or hear a thing.

The eyedrops worked wonders on Tink,
and about a week later, her beautiful eyes
opened. I will never forget that day, and my
heart will be forever touched by the way she
stared at my face, as if she was memorizing
my every feature. Tink's memories of her
hard past seemed to fade away, and her
playful spirit soon emerged. Velcro accepted
Tink immediately, and to my surprise, so did
Echo, who quickly appointed himself Tink's

personal groomer. We were a happy family.

I wish I had grabbed my camera on the day that Tink caught her first and only mouse. She proudly pranced over to show me her prize, holding her head up as high as it would go, but the poor little mouse still dragged on the ground. Not too long after Tink's grand moment, I did snap a picture of my three cats. This photograph was the one I hung on the refrigerator, the one featuring the donkey in the window. And, shortly after I saw the donkey, we surprisingly discovered an image of our loving Chance piglet standing beside the couch, in the form of her angelic self. It was incredible that not only did she love us enough to bring her smell through, she also made sure we could see her.

When we celebrated Tink's six-month-old birthday, she seemed healthy, but the scab on the back of her ear wasn't healing. We returned to the vet, and he assured me there was nothing to worry about. Still, the scab continued to grow.

Tink always curled up near our feet at bedtime, but one night she began sleeping by our front door. Shortly after her sleeping habit changed, I caught her climbing into the clay pot of one of my plants and digging in the dirt. Gently scolding her, I placed her on the ground, but she jumped back into the same plant, determined to dig again. Her unusual behavior continued until I took a closer look at the dirt and became aware of a distinct moldy smell. Apparently, the plant had been overwatered. As I dug the plant out to transfer it into a different container, I found the mold. Seeing the mold reminded me of the scab on Tink's ear. I wondered if Tink could have a fungal infection? Oddly enough, she quit digging through my plants after that.

Unfortunately, our dear farm vet was in the reserves overseas, so I helped Tink into the cat carrier and drove to the town vet yet again. Tink almost seemed relieved to be getting medical attention. When I asked the vet if the scab could have anything to do with fungus or mold, he replied, "Not in Colorado," and told me to go home. He probably thought I was being overly protective.

Days went by, and it looked to me as if Tink was agitated and becoming sicker. When I conferred with Jamie, she also thought Tink might have an infection. So I showed up at the vet's door every week, pleading for him to take a closer look. In hindsight, I realize he probably thought I was the one who was ill and not Tink. A little too late, I made the decision to look for another veterinarian, praying to find the best one for my girl.

The new veterinarian was everything I could have hoped for. She took my suggestion that Tink had an infection and ran with it. Tests were performed, and the heartbreaking results came back that same day: Tink did have a fungus, and it was growing rapidly.

The vet prescribed an extremely powerful medication, Ketoconazole, to fight the infection. With the medicine, Tink seemed to be on the mend; she even went back to lying at our feet at night. But then we found her sleeping by the front door again, and I noticed something wrong with her eyes.

Velcro stood nearby, staring at Tink, who willingly allowed me to place her in the cat carrier and sat patiently during the long ride to the vet's office. After a quick examination, the vet asked me to leave Tink at the clinic for testing. That seemed an unusual request, and I worried all the way home.

The earth-shattering phone call came that afternoon. My knees buckled when the kind vet told me that our dear little Tink's infection had gone systemic. Because it had spread to her brain, she was now blind, and it would be best for her to be euthanized.

The drive back to the clinic was a long and difficult journey. Time stood still as Al and I, the wonderful veterinarian, and her staff all gathered around precious seven-month-old Tinkerbelle. But incredibly, Tink was purring. We were astounded when we witnessed her making her way to each person in the room to be petted. It was as if, instead of being afraid, she was comforting all of us and thanking us for loving her.

Suddenly, the air in the room seemed devoid of oxygen, and I couldn't seem to catch my breath. I couldn't bear the thought of letting Tink go, but I knew I had no choice. As tears blurred my vision, the only comfort I found was that Tink would now be healed. However, as Al and I left the clinic with her precious little body, our hearts were empty.

After we buried Tink, I sat alone in my driveway. While I held the picture from the refrigerator in my hand and mourned, images of her suffering began to emerge in my thoughts. They played in an endless loop as I tried fervently to make sense of all the pain — not just the pain that Tink had endured, but the pain endured by all the dear animals, world over, that are neglected and thrown away.

Staring up at the clouds and wishing I could

have her back, I watched the sun sinking behind the mountains. As the crimson sky turned to pink and orange, I was reminded how great the universe is.

Then, a cloud in the perfect form of a cat grabbed my attention. Forming right beside it, in succession, were four other cat clouds with their tails straight up in the air. The cats appeared to be running side by side.

I thought of the painful memory of Tink purring just before she passed and my futile search for her litter mates. If there had been a litter, maybe Tink purred because she knew she was going to be with her siblings soon. As the spectacular sunset faded and the five cats in the clouds dissipated, my grief felt much lighter.

Chapter 5

Soon after I discovered the donkey and Chance in the special photograph, I found other animal faces in the picture as well. Little did I know about the blessings that were to come. Eventually, all the faces, except for that of the donkey, materialized into real animals that we adopted.

It wasn't long before the first of this mysterious batch of new animals joined our family. We adopted a two-month-old calico kitten from the local humane society. We chose a name for her that perfectly fit her demeanor: Shy.

In the photograph, the cat that bears a resemblance to Shy is on the right arm of the couch. Although Shy is not really on the couch, in the photo there seemed to be the blurry form of a calico peering out the window.

Adopting Shy was such a blessing. Although we didn't know anything about her past, I assumed it had been a hard existence because her whiskers had been cut off. Velcro easily accepted the newest member of the family, and I think Echo still missed Tink because, to our surprise, he and Shy became immediate buddies.

Now, I have heard many stories of animals rescuing their people, for example when their owner had a heart attack, or even alerting a family when their infant stopped breathing. So many times, animals have warned us in their own way of disease, the onset of an epileptic seizure or deadly changes in the weather. Other times, animals have been known to "pierce the veil of autism," as Barry Jackson describes in *Furry Paw, Middle Claw.**

I will never forget one windy night when Shy rescued us from fire. Before my family and I went to bed, Shy climbed high on top of the cupboards and shook and hid her head as if she was afraid. Then she jumped down,

**Furry Paw, Middle Claw,* a novel by Barry Jackson

went to the door, and began to meow. We didn't want to let her outside alone, so we tried consoling and coercing her, but our efforts were in vain. Despite our efforts to distract her, Shy's meows persisted like a skipping record, for at least twenty minutes, until we begrudgingly gave in and let her outside. Velcro meowed in the background, and five minutes later, the phone rang. It was our neighbors down the road calling to tell us our land was on fire.

Al and I threw on our boots, and I made a quick call to the fire department. Since we lived in the country, the firemen had a long way to go, so we grabbed gloves and shovels and raced up over the hill. The acrid scent of burning sagebrush met us at the top of the rise. As we looked down at the small, wind-driven fire, we were relieved to see a few people already there, bent over, fighting the flames with shovels. We joined the others and were able to get the fire out by the time the fire department arrived.

Al and I never knew how the fire started that night, but as we climbed wearily into our bed, we found Shy at our feet, contently curled up and back to her old self again.

Shy has even helped with the simplest, silliest problems of daily life. One time I misplaced an expensive bottle of cleaner that I used on my favorite sandals. I searched for it for weeks, to no avail. Meanwhile, Shy kept opening and closing one of the bottom cupboard doors. At first, the banging just added to my frustration, but then I had a lightbulb moment. I went to the cupboard, and when I opened it, I couldn't believe my eyes. Lo and behold, there was the cleaner. Afterwards, Shy didn't try to open that cupboard door anymore.

No matter how many times I have experienced this bond of pure love, I still am amazed at how powerful the connection can be between human beings and the animals in their care. My belief is that if Shy or Velcro or any of the animals didn't love us, they wouldn't care enough to communicate, in their own way.

Chapter 6

I thought about Chance and how much I loved her. She had been gone from our lives for a couple years, and I still really missed her. Having always had a soft spot in my heart for pigs, I thought about what it would be like to have another one around. After all, we already had a fenced-in area outside with shade, shelter, and all the other comforts a pig would enjoy.

Raising Chance had taught us a very important lesson. Our choice to adopt only one pig had resulted in Chance requiring our constant attention. Without it, she became lonely and destructive, like when she ate Mariah's homework. We didn't want to repeat the same mistake twice, so when we finally decided to adopt again, we went on a search for two piglets.

I soon found a website for a potbelly pig

sanctuary called Pig-A-Sus Homestead in Mack, Colorado. I sent an inquiring email and waited anxiously for the response.

By the next morning, the owner, Sioux, had sent an encouraging reply stating that she might have a perfect match for us. There were two black six-month-old brothers available for adoption. She explained that the two had been part of an eleven-piglet litter that had been rescued months before from Arizona. At the end of her email, Sioux warmly welcomed us to visit the sanctuary.

That Saturday, Al and I set off on our six-hour journey. When we met Sioux and her husband, Rocky, I thought how long it had been since I met such a friendly, endearing, and compassionate couple. They showed us around their many well-constructed buildings, erected with their own sweat and muscle, which, over the years, had been used to house hundreds of potbelly pigs. Then they took us to see our pig boys.

The two little ones were playful and

adorable. One of the piglets was totally black and easily took a cookie from my hand. Having picked out names before arriving, I decided to call him Mack. His brother was also black, but he had tiny white spots on his head and chest, and four little white feet. I named him Solomon. It made my heart hurt when Solomon shied away and refused the cookie that I tentatively offered him. I could tell that he was more timid than Mack, and I looked forward to the honor of building his trust.

After loading the two potbellies into the extended cab of our truck, the four of us said our goodbyes and promised to keep in touch. Then Al, Mack, Solomon and I headed off for the long ride home.

The piglets adjusted quickly to Little Feet Ranch. I was overjoyed as I listened to the oinks and happy grunts they made while they playfully chased each other in circles around the spacious pen. It wasn't too long before Solomon gingerly accepted cookies, bananas, grapes, and other scrumptious treats from my family and me. He certainly wasn't a picky pig, though we still couldn't touch him.

Mack was like a great big dog, easygoing and more sociable than his brother. One wonderful day, he allowed Al and me to give him a belly rub, letting us know that he trusted us. We felt blessed to be a part of both pigs' lives.

Years ago, we adopted a brood of chickens. They were all older now and nearing their time to cross over. One day, while doing morning chores, I noticed Solomon standing by the chicken fence with his head down. I walked over and saw he was staring at one of our grey Barred Rock chickens, who was sitting alone in the shade and looking right back at Solomon. A couple days later, our sweet old chicken passed to the Other Side and I thought of Velcro. If she could perceive when other animals were about to die, could Solomon have the same ability?

Caring for our two new pigs and our

eighteen other wonderful critters kept me so busy that I completely forgot about the special photograph. I had put it away for safekeeping, and when I came across it again, I saw that there were two more animal faces in the picture. They were at the bottom left side of the photo, huddled together, looking through the window into our house. I had seen them once before, but at that time, I couldn't quite see their distinct outline.

Now I saw they resembled the tiny, scrunched piglet faces of Mack and Solomon. Goose bumps broke out on my arms. I remembered how Nicky had appeared in my bedroom to say goodbye so many years ago. Maybe, I thought, Mack and Solomon and Shy appeared in the special photograph to say hello.

I still wondered, though, about the mysterious donkey in the window. And then I discovered a new face with piercing eyes, perched on the beanbag behind Tinkerbelle.

Chapter 7

Before the newest animal from the special photograph joined our family, Velcro, an old family member passed away. At twenty-years-old, wonderful, Velcro kitty still had a sharp mind, but her poor body was deteriorating with age. My family and I were honored to be at her side and to surround her with our love on the morning she crossed over. My heart ached for her, but I had witnessed her unique connection with the Hereafter, and I believed there was a special place reserved there, just for her.

Minutes after Velcro passed away, I heard what sounded like a faint meow. I looked over at Echo and Shy, both oblivious and sleeping comfortably on a chair. Then the phone rang. I picked up the receiver and that's when I heard the sound of a second meow. Startled and confused, I looked at the phone, and then placed the receiver down gently. I recognized the tone of that meow and without a doubt, knew for certain that it could only have come from our own, special Velcro kitty.

About a week later, while buying groceries, I came across the owner of our feed and supply store. She told me that she had rescued a pregnant cat that died soon after delivering five now helpless kittens.

In an exhausted voice, the store owner explained that she had been feeding the kittens every two hours for three weeks and they were growing like weeds. Then she asked if I could adopt one. I knew that providing a home for a kitten was the right thing to do. I said yes and promised to visit frequently during the next three weeks, after which my new kitten would be old enough to come home.

That same day, Mariah and I stopped by to visit the five precious orphans, who were as frisky and happy as could be. We couldn't help but giggle in delight at the kittens' frolicsome antics. One at a time, the store owner lifted each kitten out of the large box that served as a temporary home. The kittens had long, thin tails and were all different colors. One was tiger-striped orange, another was gray, and a third was gray and black. However, the remaining two were the ones that caught my eye.

I tickled the full tummy of a kitten that was solid black and fascinated by my touch. She stared up at me with round eyes. As the other kittens wobbled around, I noticed the last kitten sitting alone in a corner.

She had a white chin and a beautiful beige coat with orange and black spots and stripes. Sitting daintily, almost in a little pose, she reminded me of Velcro at her age. I found it hard to make a decision about which kitten to adopt because both were so perfect. But finally I chose the dainty orange-spotted kitten, and we set a date to pick her up.

About a week before we were to bring her home, while I was doing the dishes, something brushed against my leg. Thinking it was Echo or Shy, I looked down but the cats were nowhere around. The next day, while vacuuming, I saw out of the corner of my eye, a black shape flit across the floor. These mysterious experiences continued to occur sporadically until it was time to bring our new kitten home.

When Mariah and I arrived at my friend's house, we found that the kittens had already outgrown their box and were now living in a spacious room. Our kitten, who we named Meadow, was in the corner with the little black kitty. It was a picture-perfect moment: the black kitten had her arms around Meadow, and Meadow sat there kneading a blanket with her paws and sucking on the tip of her own tail. I was surprised at Meadow's behavior, but realized she acquired the tail sucking habit because she was born without a mom. Anyway, she seemed happy enough, and I hoped Meadow would be happy in her new home.

Since Meadow and the black kitten looked so happy together, I decided to adopt both of them. Mariah named the black kitty Marley. After we brought Marley home, the phantom brushes against my legs stopped, and the mysterious black shapes never returned.

Echo eventually befriended them, but Shy, who was mean to other cats, didn't change her ways for Meadow or Marley. As I petted the two kittens' soft coats, I thought of my two pigs, Mack and Solomon, and their inseparable relationship. Then I thought of our first pig, Chance, and how she had been unhappy without a companion.

As Meadow and Marley grew, so did their marvelous personalities. Meadow, with her sweet and sensitive nature, reminded me more of Velcro every day. Marley also became a joy in our lives. We laughed at her playful growling as she fetched her toy mice. And she always took time to rub against our legs just to let us know she was there.

Because the two new blessings in our family

were keeping me busy, I hadn't looked at the special photograph in a while. When I took it from the drawer, I realized I forgot about the last animal face that had appeared. The one who's piercing eyes were staring out from behind Tinkerbelle. Was it possible that the face belonged to one of the two kittens we had adopted? Could it even have been little Marley, with her bright shining eyes? If there was one thing my animal family taught me, it was that anything was possible! Then one day, the wildlife decided to teach me a lesson or two …

Chapter 8

Twice a day without fail, multiple bevies of quail explored our front yard, seeking food and water. One afternoon, the quail parents and their many babies rushed to eat before a thunderstorm hit. I noticed one baby quail off by itself. The tuft of white feathers on the baby's head bobbed rhythmically as it busily pecked the ground. The little quail seemed oblivious to the hail that was just beginning to fall.

All the birds scattered for the safety of home except for the lone baby, which had run for cover under a bush. The storm hit with full force then, but it blew over within a few minutes. Afterward, Al and I went outside to see if the baby was alright. We searched everywhere but saw no trace of the little quail. We thought maybe it had gone on its way. But then I noticed an adult quail perched on the fence near the bush in which the baby had taken shelter.

The quail was soaking wet and ruffling its feathers. We wondered why the poor bird hadn't sought shelter. Al and I went back inside the house, but I continued to watch the wet quail from the front window.

I thought perhaps the quail on the fence was the parent of the missing baby. After convincing Al to help me search again, we carefully crawled through the bushes toward the back fence. The adult quail just sat there, quietly, and observed. Then I saw the little quail lying lifeless on the ground where it had been pummeled by the hard rain. I assumed it was dead, but then the baby gasped for breath.

Al and I gently placed a dry makeshift shelter over the quail. Although the baby was very weak, its breathing quickly improved. As the sun set behind the mountains, we walked back to the house. The adult quail sat in the same spot, maybe somehow knowing its baby was alive. I said out loud that we would uncover the baby in the morning, maybe to make myself feel better. The bird didn't move. We went inside, but I continued to check on the little quail throughout the night.

As the sun rose, I looked out the window and saw, to my relief, that the parent was still there. Walking outside, I again checked the baby's progress and smiled when I saw the baby was alive and strong and hungrily pecking at the tiny seeds I left the night before.

The parent sat unmoving on the fence while I tiptoed back inside. What I witnessed next was amazing. The adult quail flew down onto the ground, landing in front of the baby. Immediately, the baby scampered over to the parent. They sat there for a few minutes, and then the parent stood and scrambled away, with the baby following close behind.

I was grateful for the happy ending. It was incredible to see the survival instinct of the baby and the profound love and determination of the parent.

Afterword

I could go on and on about how all animals are extraordinary creatures. In fact, just recently, my goat Chloe did something that reminded me of the story of a dog, who would lay at his owner's grave every night.

Chloe was a miniature goat and had two sons, one was velvet black, named Jake and the other had a beautiful coat that reminded me of an antelope. His name was Oliver. Unexpected in an animal so young, our Jake died. I knelt and put my arms around Chloe and Oliver, trying to comfort them with soothing words, "Jake is okay and when it's both your times to pass, you can be with him."

Oliver didn't seem to care what I said, but Chloe looked from me to Jake then stood quietly nearby, studying our every move, as we buried Jake in the critter cemetery. My poor mother goat vigilantly stared at the cemetery for two days and only took short breaks to eat and drink a little water. To say the least, I was worried about Chloe, and what was even more peculiar was that she looked worried, too.

I remembered what I told Chloe while she watched us bury her kid. The words, "It's okay and when it's your time to pass, you can be with him," replayed in my mind. I believed that animals could understand languages and when I saw Chloe's worried pacing and exhaustion, I knew Chloe thought she had to go into the ground to be with Jake. So I repeated that Jake was okay and rephrased what would happen when she crossed over. After she settled down and went back to her daily routine of being her unique self, I was more careful of what I said around the animals.

I am honored and humbled to have learned so much from the animals and to have experienced their unconditional love. I am certain their intuition and ways of communication aren't so different from ours. Just as we use eyes and ears to reach out and explore the world around us, we can use our hearts and minds to create connections that can last a lifetime and beyond.

Yes, the amazing stories never end, and although I still don't know where the donkey came from in my special photograph, I respect that just as people can be Angels on earth or the Other Side, so can animal companions. Because Angels really do come in all shapes and sizes!

ACKNOWLEDGEMENTS

From elephants and seals to birds, cats, dogs, fish, and mice, here is a special acknowledgement to some of our Angel Friends on Earth and the Other Side.

Nicholas James, Flower, Leasha, Fudgie, Christmas, Jamid, P.J., Alex, Velcro, Corkscrew, Tory, Raven, Magic, Opus, Buzz and Missy, Echo, D.O.G., Teddy, Hermy, Fighter fishes, Fire belly newts, Peter, Osage and Capra, Phyllis, Baby Huey, Clint, Mojo, Blanca, Quarrion, Triton, Jazz, Rodeo, Fire belly newts, Oscar, Jack, Pleco, Moo Cow, Chance, Dan, Tinkerbelle, Shy, Mack and Solomon, Chloe, Jake, Oliver, Morris, Meadow and Marley, Rufus, Memory, Henry, Jo Lee, Wilbur, Cottontail bunnies, Quail, Goldie, Mickey, Sweet Pea, Echo, Luna, Bandito, Hammy, Snitch, Angel, Buster, Clarence, Cow Cat, Annie, Precious, Tequila, Thomas, Orange Cat, Whiskers, Figaro, Catnip, Buttercup, Petunia, Daisy, Dandelion, Big Red, Buddy, Thumbelina, Frodo, Griswold, Pookah, Patches, Pasha, Chloe, Black Jack, Bugsy, Junior, Cody, Sheila, Mariah, Mocha, Vanilla, Latte, Booger, Monster, Bandit, Napoleon, Samantha, Coco, Smoky, Shady, Polly, Peru, Becky, Gidget, Mimi, Remy, Christina, Elvis, Thumper , L.J., Swamper, Rye, Lola, Daisy, Pearlie Jo, Hecky, Sassy, Chandler, Jordan, Elf, Sunny, Gypsy, Cleo, Bo, Lucky, Sandy, Amy, Crackers, Keeper, Buddy, Outlaw, Angel, Minnie Mouse, Blackie, Mouse, Smokey, Welcome Kitty, Sprat, Rusty, Stryker, Ziggy, Joe Cocker, Zildjian, Watogla Wanji, Jessie, Jake, Muffy, Lefty, Cocoa, Calista, T.C., Nicodemus, Pepper, Tiki, Lulu Lucy, Lizzy, Rufus, Satin, Church, Sebastian, Mousie, Cleo, Cosmo-Daisy, Hamish MacBeth, Hajji Baba, Padma Moonflower, Lakshmi, Bona, Baby, Mittens, Muffin, Buddy, Lady Pandora, Ursa, Earnie the Hemmingway Cat, Sparky, Stormy, Unser, Stanley, Speckles, Peppy, and Happy.

Light and Love
Honor the animals
whether they have paws, hooves,
fins, or can fly . . .
Say a prayer to cherish and thank them
for their sacrifices and Light.
And know how blessed you are,
when they allow you to gaze into their eyes,
to see the look of unconditional Love
that's meant to be a precious gift
sent down from up above!

Hevine Schmidt

About the Author

Hevine Schmidt lives in Colorado, where she was raised. She was a former member of search and rescue and a volunteer Firefighter I/EMT.

Now she enjoys spending time with her human and animal family at Little Feet Ranch, and is working on a children's series and a novel.

Hevine is also the author of an inspiring true story titled *Every Precious Moment*, which she created as a heartfelt tribute to everyone battling cancer.

If you are interested in making a donation to help animals, please donate to Pig-A-Sus Homestead, (featured on Animal Planet) or Western Colorado Potbelly Pig Education Health Center. Visit Sioux Robbins-Bartels at www.pigasus.org.

Pig-A-Sus Homestead
506 S. Road
Mack, Colorado 81525
(970) 858-9628

Jazz

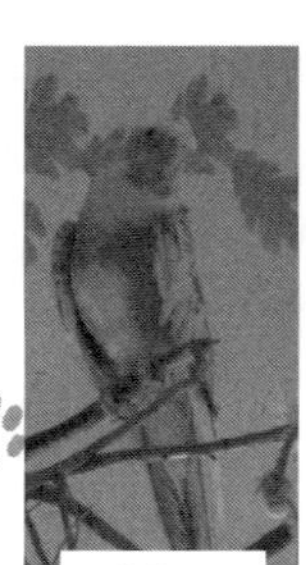

Mojo

Chloe

Oliver

Echo

Velcro Kittty

D.O.G.

Missy, Buzz, Chivo, Osage and Capra

Meadow and Marley

Tinkerbelle

Donkey in the window

Chance

Rufus

Solomon and Mack